A Lazy Cook's Christmas

mouthwatering recipes
for the time-pressured cook

created by

Lazy Cook Mo Smith

®

A Lazy Cook's Christmas

this edition published in August 2002

by

Lazy Cook Mo Smith
Bear House
Bisley
Glos.
GL6 7BB

Tel: 01452 770298
E-mail: info@lazycookmosmith.co.uk
Website: www.lazycookmosmith.co.uk

ISBN 0-9542319-2-9

Written, Edited and Published by
Lazy Cook Mo Smith

First published in October 1999, under the title
'Enter the New Millennium with Lazy Cook Mo Smith',
by BriCor (ISBN 1-902100-24-7)

Acknowledgements
Mary Rudd – Historical Records of Bisley
Cover Design by Terry Cripps, Stroud, Glos.
Printed by: Leckhampton Printing Co., Cheltenham, Glos.

Written and Published by the same author

'A Lazy Cook's Summer'
ISBN 0-9542319-0-2
£6.99 per copy
(a percentage from each sale is given to charity)

'Lazy Cook in the Kitchen'
ISBN 0-9542319-1-0
£6.99 per copy
(a percentage from each sale is given to charity)

Copies available from

Lazy Cook Mo Smith
Bear House
Bisley
Glos.
GL6 7BB
Tel: 01452 770298
E-mail: info@lazycookmosmith.co.uk
Website: www.lazycookmosmith.co.uk

*(Cheques made payable to **Lazy Cook Mo Smith**)*

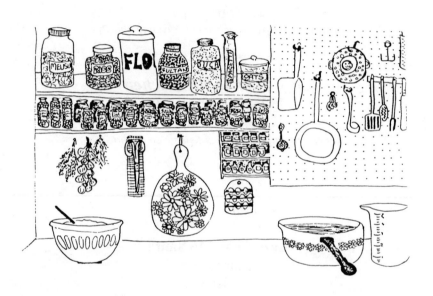

Contents

Bear House

Bisley over the past 1000 years - a potted history

"where do you come from - Bisley, God help us"
Bisley old saying

I feel very privileged to have lived in Bisley since 1973. To me it is one of the most beautiful parts of this Cotswold plateau. It's ancient buildings of unusual architecture, it's narrow winding streets and pathways and it's fascinating history dating back as far as the Neolithic age give Bisley a uniqueness and a charm of it's very own. As I sit in my kitchen at Bear House, which itself dates back to the 16th century I think of the people who lived here before me. As I gaze through my kitchen window at the natural grey stone of neighbouring cottages, the picturesque facade of the Bear Inn, the ancient lock-ups and the majestic church steeple, I wonder what it would have been like to have lived in Bisley a thousand years or more ago. What were the lifestyles of the inhabitants of Bisley? And of greater interest to me as a cook, what, I wonder, were their eating habits, from where did their ingredients come and how were they cooked?

"Bisley gates are open" - when the wind blows from the north.
Bisley old saying

History books tell us that the years 1000-1500, the Middle Ages, was a time of great poverty, but rich and poor alike would have lived without many of the things we now take for granted. For instance, a house or dwelling place would have consisted of just one room where the whole family lived, cooked, ate and slept. There would have been no sheet glass for window panes, simply openings in a wall, letting in wind and driving rain as readily as they did light and air. In winter, heating and light were not provided by the pressing of a switch, a pottery vessel containing a lighted wick set in oil gave light, and heating came from an open fire in the centre of the room. There was no chimney, just a small hole in the roof which frequently filled the room with smoke when the wind blew. However, this fire was essential not only for warmth but for cooking.

While the basic principles of cooking were similar to those of today, the facilities and equipment could not be compared with the luxury of the four-oven Aga which adorns my kitchen, and the ingredients we all take for granted today. Roads were poor, there were no cars and certainly no maze of motorways along which to transport ingredients from all corners of the globe. There were neither supermarkets nor village stores - ingredients came from the land, in the form of vegetables, wild berries and pulses and, on rare occasions, meat.

> "And further see old Bisley spire
> Which rises quite as high or higher
> Than most in Gloucestershire.
> And thousands round that ancient pile
> Lie mouldering till the Seventh Vial
> I poured upon the air"
> Bisley old saying

Bisley, at this time would have consisted of the church and Overcourt. The latter would have been known as the Manor but it would not have resembled the fine building we see today. There would have been numerous barns belonging to the Manor and humble cottages for the estate workers. Outside the inhabited area would have been agricultural and grazing land for sheep.

> "Beggarley Bisley, Strutting Stroud,
> Mincing Hampton, Painswick proud"
> Bisley old saying

Bisley during this period was a town, a town of importance and size. It was an area which included the parishes of Stroud, Painswick, Misserden, Edgeworth, Winstone and Sapperton with Frampton Mansell, forming what was, and is still referred to, as the 'Bisley Hundred', one of the seven hundreds of Cirencester. (i)

The origin of the name Bisley is believed to have been taken from natural objects - 'bisse' a doe, and 'leah' a pasture. It is interesting to recall some of the changes that were made to the spelling of the name over the centuries from Biseleg to Bisseleye and the present day spelling which came about during the reign of Queen Elizabeth I.

(i) A form of government brought in by the Anglo-Saxons gathering people into households and into hundreds. The tendency was to concentrate the rural Inhabitants in villages or 'tuns' for safety.

"These poor sheep have nothing to shelter them but Bisley spire"
- a saying at Stow-on-the-Wold

The industrial revolution brought exciting change for Bisley and indeed for England and the world. The superior quality of the fleeces from sheep which grazed on the Cotswold hills had long been recognised and the export of this wool to the continent became a lucrative business. Most of the weaving until this time had been done in cottages or in the houses of master weavers, but gradually all cottage weaving ceased and was replaced by mills whose machinery did the job more quickly and efficiently. Fortunes were made and lost and the development of Bisley as we see it today evolved.

However, the poor and homeless still suffered and a workhouse was opened in Joiners Lane. It is recorded that the inmates were 'stript and cleaned and new clothed'. They were fed on a diet of broth thickened with oatmeal. Milk, pease and onion pottage and, if they behaved, they were given bread and a small beer for breakfast and supper. Even so, there was to be no supper for those who 'swear or curse, or behave disorderly or break open a gate'.

Frequent outbreaks of smallpox and fever occurred and eventually a 'pest' house was opened at Oakridge where such cases could be treated in isolation. The human misery and disease experienced by these inmates is unbelievably sad and death offered the sole means of escape. Nature does her best each returning spring and clothes their nameless graves in a covering of snowdrops reflecting a purity and beauty which was so sadly lacking in the lives of so many.

'Requiescant in pace - let them rest in peace'.

As I walk through the churchyard each spring, the sight of the snowdrops brings thoughts of the past and of the sad and hard lives of many. It is a humbling experience.

But here my reverie must cease if I am to complete this short history of Bisley. As a cook it is the changes in the diets of both rich and poor over the past one thousand years which is of prime interest to me.

A thousand years ago the families of those in agricultural work would have been provided with a cottage with a garden where vegetables and herbs were grown. A few animals would also have been kept for simple family needs - an ox, cows or goats, a few sheep, pigs and chickens. The ox would have been the work animal. The sheep might have been milked but would more likely have been kept for their fleeces. The hens provided eggs. Cockerels and pigs were the only animals kept for meat and poultry but it is doubtful these would have provided nourishing meals for the family, they would more likely have been sold at market, as would the fleeces.

> "pease pudding hot
> pease pudding cold
> pease pudding in the pot
> nine days old"
> Traditional rhyme

Ninety per cent of the population of Bisley lived in poverty such as we cannot begin to imagine. The diet of many families would have been plain and monotonous consisting mostly of pease pudding or pottage - a thick soup of home-grown vegetables and possibly a scant trace of meat. A heavy bread and cheese, both home-made, might have provided a mid-day meal. In the autumn fruit and nuts would have been stored or pickled and meat salted or smoked for preservation, but again most of these items would have been sold at market rather than enjoyed by these very poor, undernourished families.

By contrast, a landowners diet would have included meat, fruit and spices, eggs, bread and milk, pastries, cheeses and several varieties of fish, from fishcakes to oysters, and the best roasts including venison and other game. Nibbles and aperitifs, hogsheads of wine and kegs of beer would also have been served with evening meals. Any leftovers would be put into a 'dole' or 'poor' cupboard.

It is clear to me from the foregoing that many of the ingredients used over the centuries are not dissimilar from those used today. It is the availability of such varied ingredients, the preparation and the methods of cooking nowadays which are so very different.

Strange as it may seem, I believe our ancestors had certain advantages over us in this new millennium. Whilst ready made meals and takeaways were unheard of, neither were sell-by dates, B.S.E. and G.M. Both rich and poor enjoyed the luxury of vegetables grown in rich natural soil, picked fresh from the garden and put straight into the pot. We pay dearly for such ingredients today under the heading 'organically grown'.

Another change which has come about over the centuries, but of much importance, is that of time. For the poor life moved at a slow, monotonous pace. For the wealthy landowners and the new era of mill owners life was ever changing. With their newly acquired wealth large houses were built where entertaining was arranged on a lavish scale. Extravagant dinners, balls, weekend house and shooting parties became popular and all had to be catered for. This gave employment to many but, without the modern equipment of today, the work was hard and the payment a pittance.

"There is nothing new under the sun"
Ecclesiastes Ch.I v.8

And so it seems we have turned full circle in this new millennium. The trendy gardeners of today plant cabbages, lettuces and beans on sticks amongst their flower-beds. In extreme cases lawns are dug up and replaced by small fruit trees and vegetables of every kind in order that a family can once again become self-sufficient and eat chemical-free produce.

Modern refrigeration, microwaves, washing machines and shopping on the internet have replaced the armies of servants provided by our ancestors and once so vital to the smooth running of big houses. Life below stairs has been replaced by life on the factory floor packing ready-made meals, filling tins, jars and bags with fresh and frozen ingredients, all for our convenience. Attractively packaged for display on the supermarket shelf where they wait to be snapped up by today's time-pressured cook.

My 'Lazy Cook' recipes, a handful of which I promote in this book, are created for living in this new century as they are ideally suited to the rapidly changing and busy lifestyle of today's cook.

Introduction to Recipes

*"On the first day of Christmas my true love sent to me -
a partridge in a pear tree"*
Traditional rhyme

I have always responded to the challenge of mixing a handful of ingredients and creating a new flavour. It began when I was a very small child. One of my earliest memories is of the Christmas when the family were given a huge box of chocolates. This was a selection box of the type shops displayed and from which the amount requested was weighed, provided you had enough ration coupons, as well as money to buy them.

After the family's initial enjoyment of this luxury on Christmas Day, the box was stored on the stairs in our tiny house. 'Yours truly' spent the following days 'playing' all alone, in my parents bedroom. What I was actually doing was creeping downstairs at regular intervals, selecting a handful of chocolates and when safely back in the bedroom, carefully removing the centres and mixing them to create new flavours. The proof of the pudding is in the eating and I ate a lot of chocolates. You might imagine the trouble I was in when the much depleted box of chocolates was discovered. But the punishment didn't deter me and I have spent a lifetime experimenting with ingredients and creating new and original flavours. I have also studied the many changes in cooking over the years and I believe my 'Lazy Cook' range of recipes are ideally suited to today's busy lifestyle.

Life is too short to spend unnecessary time in the kitchen especially at Christmas and the selection of 'Lazy Cook' recipes I give in this book will help you over the busy Christmas holiday and beyond.

My recipes promote healthy eating and are made from many 'off the shelf' and store cupboard ingredients. Quick and easy to prepare they can be made by the least experienced cook, they will entice the least enthusiastic cook into the kitchen and the most talented cook will discover new recipes to add to their repertoire - whatever the occasion my 'Lazy Cook' recipes, tips and anecdotes will leave you with time and energy to enjoy it.

Menus and Recipes

I have divided the recipes in this book into sections to suit any entertaining you may be planning over the Christmas period but they can, of course, be switched about to suit your day to day catering throughout the year.

'Come for a weekend'

'A Lazy Cook's Christmas day'

'Boxing Day - a meal after a walk'

'Let's have a party!'

'New Year's Eve dinner party'

Come for a weekend!

It is not unusual for me to invite visitors for a weekend just before Christmas. It seems to me a good time to get together with family or friends, a time to relax and to reflect and to gently get into the rhythm of Christmas, and I can think of no better place to do this than round a table, sharing a meal.

The 'Lazy Cook' recipes I have selected for such a weekend will enable you to serve meals which look attractive and taste good but take the minimum of time to prepare. Careful shopping and just a little preparation before the visitors arrive will be time well spent and will ensure a happy and relaxed weekend for everyone.

Weekend Menus

Friday

Evening dinner

Oyster mushrooms on oven-baked toast with a fresh coriander garnish

Salmon steaks with baked red peppers served with a savoury orange sauce

Pasta twists

Baked celery hearts with fresh lemon and sage

Blackcurrant trifle

Cheeseboard - your own personal selection

Coffee

Chocolate and almond fudge

Saturday

Lunch

Warm savoury cheesecake with a goats cheese topping

Winter salad

Bread or rolls

Fresh fruit - a seasonal selection

Coffee

Tea

Iced gingerbread

Oatcake

Dinner

Baked tomatoes with a savoury filling

Ham with mustard sauce

Quick cauliflower cheese

Small potatoes baked in their jackets

Cinnamon shortbread

Cheeseboard

Coffee

Chocolate peppermint creams

Sunday

Brunch

Kedgeree

Fruit butter tart

Cheeseboard - of your own choice

Coffee

Friday evening dinner

Oyster mushrooms on oven-baked toast with a fresh coriander garnish - serves 4

200gms (8ozs) oyster mushrooms
4ozs white wine
few spots mushroom ketchup
1 tbls cream
freshly ground white pepper
4 slices thick-sliced bread
butter
a few sprigs fresh coriander

Wipe the mushrooms with damp kitchen paper. Heat the wine and mushroom ketchup in a large pan, add the mushrooms and simmer gently, with lid on pan for 5mins. stir in the cream and freshly ground pepper and keep warm. Remove the crusts from the bread, butter the slices and bake until brown in the oven or under a grill, put on to individual hot plates and cover with the mushrooms. Spoon the sauce over and garnish with fresh coriander, serve.

Useful tips - for good presentation use large mushrooms if you are able to buy them.

Salmon steaks with baked red peppers served with a savoury orange sauce - serves 4

2 red peppers
Olive oil
4 salmon steaks
freshly ground white pepper
5 ozs dry white wine
5 ozs orange juice (from a carton)
1 teas. sundried tomato puree
100gms (4ozs) gorgonzola (or a strong blue cheese)

Set the oven at gas 6/450f/220c/Aga roasting oven Remove the top from the peppers and the seeds and centre pink ~ flesh. Cut in half lengthways and put into an ovenproof dish (skin side up) and brush well with olive oil, place in pre-set oven and roast until brown (about 30mins). Make the sauce by putting the wine and orange juice into a pan, boil for a few minutes to reduce a little, add the tomato puree and the cheese, crumbled into pieces, and whisk until the cheese has melted into the sauce. Bring back to a simmer, remove from heat, place lid on pan. Using a sharp knife remove the bone from each steak (these can be used for a fish stock, recipe on page 50). Brush each steak with oil and season with pepper, place in an ovenproof dish and bake for 3-4mins. on each side, remove from oven and keep warm. To serve, place the steaks down the centre of a serving dish. Using scissors make several cuts down each pepper half, place on top of each steak opening them like a fan. Bring the sauce back to a simmer and pour a little round the steaks, serve the remainder separately. Serve with pasta and a seasonal vegetable.

Useful tips - both the peppers and the steaks can be cooked on the top of the cooker or under a grill. The length of cooking time depends on the thickness of the steaks. The sauce can be made with a simple fish stock instead of wine (recipe below).

Fish stock - put the fish bones into a small pan with a few peppercorns, a bayleaf and a squeeze of lemon juice. Simmer, with lid on pan, for 30mins. Strain before use. When cold this stock can be frozen. I find the flavour of bought fish stock is often too overpowering for the other ingredients.

Pasta
Choose the type of pasta you like, fresh or dried and cook it following the manufacturers instructions.

Baked celery hearts with fresh lemon and sage - serves 4
2 celery hearts
1 lemon
fresh or dried sage

Cut the celery hearts into 6-8 lengths and boil in a little water until they begin to soften. Strain off the cooking liquid and toss the celery in lemon zest, a little lemon juice and sage. Transfer to a vegetable dish to serve.

Useful tips - instead of buying celery hearts which can be quite expensive, I buy 2 heads of celery and cut off the tops to within l2cms (5") of the hearts. Cook the hearts as in the above recipe and use the remaining sticks in winter salads and soups.

Blackcurrant trifle - serves 6-8

1 pkt trifle sponges
1 jar (680gms) blackcurrants in syrup
5 ozs double cream
shavings of bitter chocolate for decoration

Split the trifle sponges and put half of them into a trifle dish, cover with half the blackcurrants and some juice, top with the remaining trifle sponges, blackcurrants and juice. Allow the juice to penetrate the sponges before spreading with lightly whipped cream and scattering with shavings of bitter chocolate to serve.

Useful tips - make in advance and add the cream to serve. It is made in about 5mins. - very "Lazy Cook", very delicious.

Coffee making

There are many different blends of coffee and coffee making equipment on the market to choose from but I still prefer to make fresh coffee in an earthenware jug, rather like making tea. From a Coffee and Tea Merchant in Stroud, I buy a blend of Kenya and French beans, equal quantities of each, mixed. I store them in the fridge.

To make 1 ltr (2pts) jug of fresh coffee, grind 2 tbls. beans and put into the jug. Fill with water, preferably just off the boil, stir well, put lid on jug and leave for 5mins. before pouring through a sieve. I consider this to be the quickest, the cheapest and far the best way to enjoy fresh coffee.

Chocolate and almond fudge

Recipe on page 30/31.

Saturday Lunch

Warm savoury cheesecake with goats cheese topping - 6-8 slices

100gms (4ozs) self-raising flour
1 teas. caster sugar
3 size 1 eggs
100gms (4ozs) full fat cream cheese
1 jar sundried tomatoes in olive oil
50gms (2ozs) pitted black olives
freshly ground white pepper
300gms (12ozs) goats cheese - for topping

Set oven at gas 4/400f/200c/Aga baking oven
Put a paper cake-baking case into an 18cm (7") round cake tin (or line with oiled greaseproof). Put the flour, sugar, eggs and cheese into a food processor and process until smooth. Add 6 sundried tomatoes, the olives and pepper and process for a few seconds to mix in. Pour into prepared tin and bake in pre-set oven for 25-30mins. or until set. Allow to cool a little before topping with sundried tomatoes and covering with slices of goats cheese. Put back into the oven, or under a grill, until the goats cheese has melted. Remove from paper case and slice to serve.

Useful tips - I freeze this cheesecake whole or in slices. To serve, defrost and add the sundried tomatoes and goats cheese as directed above. Alternatively it can be served by spreading the top thickly with cream or curd cheese seasoned with lots of fresh parsley, then garnish with radish flowers, spring onions or any salad ingredient. It is a most unusual cheesecake, very light and good to eat. Small slices can be served as a starter or added to a platter of cold meats. Made in a square tin it can be thickly spread with seasoned cream cheese, cut into small cubes and served at a drinks party along with other tasty canapes.

Winter salad
Mix together watercress, sliced celery, sliced spring onions, chopped carrot, radish halves, sliced Chinese leaves and a little grated parsnip. Serve with oil and vinegar dressing (recipe below)

Oil and vinegar dressing/vinaigrette
Whisk 4ozs oil with 1oz wine or cider vinegar and freshly ground pepper

Home-made bread the "Lazy Cook" way
make it - shape it - rise it - bake it

Bread - household white
400gms (1lb) strong white flour
1 teas. salt (optional)
13gms (half an ounce) fresh yeast
1 teas. sugar
10ozs (half pint) warm water

Set oven at gas 7/475f/230c/Aga roasting oven. Cream the yeast and sugar together with a little warm water, stir in the remaining water to make up to 10ozs (half a pint). Put the flour and salt into a food processor and process for a few seconds before adding the liquid yeast mixture, switch off as soon as a dough is formed. Remove from the machine on to a lightly floured surface and knead until it becomes a smooth, waxy texture. Shape into a loaf and place on to a lightly greased and floured baking sheet, or place in a loaf tin which has been lightly greased and floured. Put to rise and when it has doubled in size bake in the pre-set oven for 20-30 mins. remove from oven, tap the base and if it sounds hollow the loaf is baked, if not return it to the oven for further baking. Leave to cool on a wire tray.

To make by hand, mix the flour and salt together in a large bowl. Cream the yeast with the sugar and water as described above, add to the flour and mix by hand into a dough. Turn on to a lightly floured surface and knead, shape, rise and bake as above.

Useful tips - although bread making is not usually associated with "lazy cooking" prepared as described above it really is a very quick process, especially if you enjoy the added luxury of an Aga. The texture and flavour of this dough can be changed in many ways, for example add 30gms or an ounce of lard, butter or margarine, an egg, or use a mixture of milk and water. It can also be shaped into rolls (when 25gms (1oz) fresh yeast will be needed), or used as a pizza base. The warmth of the kitchen will be sufficient to rise the dough, it will even rise if put into a polythene bag and placed in a fridge. The longer the dough takes to rise the better the texture will be. Fresh yeast can be stored in a fridge for a few days, or frozen. If dried yeast is used follow the instructions on the packet, I think dried yeast produces a loaf dry in texture. I have given a recipe using just 400gms (1lb) flour but larger quantities can be mixed. 25gms (1 oz) fresh yeast will be sufficient to rise a 1200gms (3 lbs) quantity of strong flour. This bread is suitable for freezing.

Bread - wholemeal
200 gms (8ozs) strong white flour
200 gms (8ozs) wholemeal flour
half teas. salt (optional)
13gms (half ounce) fresh yeast
1 teas sugar
1 tbls. oil
1 dessert. molasses
a good 10ozs (half pint) warm water

Make up following the method described in the household white bread recipe stirring the oil and molasses into the liquid yeast mixture.

Useful tips - wholemeal flour absorbs more liquid than white flour and you may find 11ozs of yeast liquid will be needed to make a smooth, pliable dough - the dough will not rise if it is too dry. Suitable for freezing.

Tea

Iced gingerbread
200 gms (8 ozs) plain flour
half teas. bicarbonate of soda
half teas. mixed spice
half teas. ground ginger
100 gms (4ozs) butter - melted
3 tbls. black treacle
1 tbls. golden syrup
5ozs milk
2 size 1 eggs
topping - optional
200 gms (8ozs) icing sugar
1 egg white
a selection of chopped walnuts, glacé cherries and crystallised ginger

Set oven at gas 3/300f/150c/Aga simmering oven.
Line the base and sides of 1kg (2lb) loaf tin with greaseproof, and grease. Put the flour, spice, ginger and bi-carb. into a food processor and process for a few seconds. Add the remaining ingredients and process until smooth. Pour into the prepared tin, stand it on a baking sheet and bake in the pre-set oven until set, 1-2hrs. Remove from tin and cool on a wire tray. Make up the icing to spreadable consistency and spread all over the top of the gingerbread then cover with the chopped fruit, nuts and ginger. Leave to set before cutting.

Useful tip - store with or without the topping in an airtight tin, eat within 5 days. This gingerbread freezes well, add the topping after thawing. I think gingerbread is a lovely cake to serve at Christmas.

Oat cake
100 gms (4ozs) margarine
75gms (3ozs) self-raising flour
100 gms (4ozs) porridge oats
50gms (2ozs) demerera sugar

Set oven at gas 4/400f/200c/Aga baking oven.
Lightly oil an 18cms (7") sandwich tin. Melt the margarine in a large pan over a gentle heat. Remove from heat and add the remaining ingredients, mix well. Press into the prepared tin and bake for 30-40 mins. in the pre-set oven. Cut into slices while still hot. When cold store in an airtight tin.

Useful tips - I first remember eating this when I was a child and it is a flavour that has remained with me ever since. It was made by a relative who recently passed the recipe on to me. Make double the quantity and press into a swiss roll tin and cut into wedges. It also makes an interesting base to top with whipped cream and fresh fruit as a pudding, or as a base for one of the many varieties of cheese-cake - it is very good.

Dinner

Baked tomatoes with a savoury filling - serves 4.
4 fresh, round tomatoes
50gms (2ozs) breadcrumbs (fresh or dried)
4 dried apricots

4 anchovy fillets
a few pinches herbs de Provence
2 teas. fresh lemon juice
freshly ground white pepper
a little sweet sherry
fresh salad leaves for garnish

Set oven at gas 4/400f/200c/Aga baking oven. Slice the rounded end from
each tomato and scoop out the pips and centre flesh, reserve any juice. Make
a filling by putting the breadcrumbs, apricots, anchovy fillets, herbs, lemon juice
and pepper into a food processor or liquidiser, adding any reserved tomato
juice, and process until it forms a sticky texture (a little sweet sherry
should be added if the filling is too dry). Pack this into the prepared tomato
cases and place lids on top. Put into a lightly oiled shallow, ovenproof dish
and bake in the pre-set oven for 20-30mins or until the tomatoes have
softened. Serve hot, warm or cold with a few fresh salad leaves and a little
vinaigrette (recipe on page 13).

Useful tips - by slicing the rounded end from the tomatoes they will sit firmly in
the dish when filled.

Ham with mustard sauce - to serve 4
1 450g jar mustard piccalilli
1 180g jar cocktail onions
2 ozs milk
5 ozs stock - ham if available
a little clear honey
4 thick slices of cooked ham

Empty the piccalilli into a pan with 10-12 cocktail onions but not vinegar. Add
the milk and stock (whisking if necessary to prevent curdling), and bring to boil
then reduce to a simmer. Sweeten to taste with clear honey. Add the ham
slices and simmer for a few minutes. To serve arrange the ham slices down
the centre of a serving dish and pour a little sauce over, serve the remaining
sauce separately.

Useful tips - this is one of the quickest meals I prepare and one of the most
enjoyed. It is a useful sauce which can be served with fish or poultry, rice or
pasta and any remaining can be added to soup. It should be stored in a

covered container in a fridge. I also prepare this recipe using a home-cooked ham or bacon joint, it takes a little longer to prepare but it is well worth the effort. Some of the stock can be used in the mustard sauce and the remainder can be frozen for future use in soups and sauces.

To boil a ham or bacon joint
Put the joint into a large pan, cover with cold water and leave to soak for 1-2 hrs. Strain off the water and discard. Cover the joint with fresh cold water, place over a low heat, without lid. Bring slowly to a gentle simmer (an occasional bubble), skim the top then add 2 dried bayleaves, 10 whole cloves and one tablespoon demerera sugar. Cover and allow to simmer "gently" for one hour (this can be done in the simmering oven of an Aga). Remove pan from heat and leave the joint in the stock for 30mins. before serving hot or cold.

Useful tips - although this method says "to boil", boiling is not recommended, it should " gently simmer" throughout the cooking.

Quick cauliflower cheese - serves 4
1 cauliflower
150gms (6ozs) grated cheese (a mixture of Stilton and Cheddar)
50gms (2ozs) jumbo oats

Break the cauliflower into small florets and wash. Add to a pan of boiling water and boil until beginning to soften. Using a slotted spoon put into a shallow ovenproof dish and add 3-4tbls. of the cooking liquid. Mix the cheeses and oats together and put on top of the cauliflower. Brown under a hot grill or a hot oven - Aga roasting oven.

Useful tips - the cauliflower can be cooked and stored, covered, in a fridge, use within 3 days. Breadcrumbs can be used instead of oats. This is a "Lazy Cook" alternative to the traditional cauliflower cheese.

Potatoes baked in their jackets
Set oven gas 6/450f/220c/Aga roasting oven. Scrub potatoes, mark with an x and bake in the pre-set oven for an hour or until crisp. Serve hot with butter.

Potato halves baked in their jackets

Set oven gas 6/450f/220c/Aga roasting oven.
Scrub the potatoes and cut in half. Brush the cut side with oil and cover with freshly grated nutmeg. Bake in the pre-set oven for an hour or until crisp.

Useful tips - these halves look a little more delicate to serve than whole potatoes. Nutmeg is an excellent flavouring for potatoes.

Cinnamon Shortbread - serves 4-6

4 shortbread plates - recipe below
10ozs double cream
1 teas. cinnamon powder
shavings of bitter chocolate

Add the cinnamon to the cream and whip to a soft peak. Sandwich the shortbread plates together with the cream and spread the remainder on top and scatter with shavings of bitter chocolate.

Useful tips - make chocolate shavings by cutting down a piece of chocolate using a sharp knife.

Shortbread plates - makes 4

100gms (4ozs) butter - softened
50gms (2ozs) caster sugar
125gms (5ozs) plain flour
25gms (1oz) ground rice

Set oven at gas 4/400f/200c/Aga baking oven.
Cream the butter and sugar together until a light fluffy consistency. Add the flour and ground rice and mix to a smooth paste. Cut into 4 pieces and roll each piece between sheets of greaseproof paper into a round approximately 20cms (8") in diameter. Place on baking sheet and bake for 6-8mins. or until they turn a light biscuit colour. Cool on a wire tray, remove paper to serve.

Chocolate Peppermint Creams

Recipe on page 31.

Sunday Brunch

Kedgeree - serves 4-6
400gms (1 lb) rice - boiled
400gms (1 lb) smoked haddock
1 large onion - skin and chop
1 tbls. oil
4 eggs - hard boil, shell and chop
freshly ground pepper
1 tbls. freshly chopped parsley
5ozs single cream

Put the haddock into a pan of boiling water, bring to simmer, remove from heat, put lid on pan and leave for 5 mins. Remove the haddock and flake (discard water). Soften the onion in hot oil, add all remaining ingredients and stir until hot. Serve.

Useful tips - Kedgeree is traditionally served in some households for breakfast on Boxing day. It can be made with brown or white rice and cream or butter can be stirred in during the final heating. The rice, haddock and eggs can be prepared a day or two in advance (store, covered, in the fridge), and the meal can then be assembled for serving very quickly.

Fruit butter tart - serves 6-8
1 cooked pastry case 16cms (7")
75gms (3ozs) butter
50gms (2ozs) demerera sugar
200gms (8ozs) mixed dried fruit
3 size 1 eggs - whisk together

Set oven at gas mark 4/400f/200c/Aga baking oven. Melt the butter and stir in the sugar, remove from heat and add the dried fruit and the eggs and mix together. Pour into the cooked pastry case, stand on a baking tray and bake in the preset oven for 20-30mins, or until set and the top is browning. Serve hot, warm or cold with single cream or ice cream.

Useful tips - I keep in a good store of cooked pastry cases, available from most supermarkets. They are a marvellous standby for making the above pudding or for a quick savoury or sweet flan - very "Lazy Cook".

A 'Lazy Cook's' Christmas Day

We are fortunate that our Christmas day is still very much a family occasion shared with aunts and uncles, nieces and nephews and the new generation of children and toddlers. We keep up the family traditions remembered from our own youth - morning church, the turkey with all the trimmings, the room darkened for the ceremonial entry of the 'flaming' Christmas pudding, home-made chocolates with coffee, the Queen's speech then a walk. After tea Father Christmas brings presents and so the day progresses - some watch the James Bond, others reminisce and we all come together for a game before supper.

Despite all this activity and the many meals and the extra little luxuries expected on Christmas day, my duties as head cook are reduced to roasting the turkey and cooking the sprouts. 'How can this be so?' you may ask. Take a look through my Christmas day menus, read the recipes and the useful tips given with them and you will discover how easy it is to enjoy a traditional family Christmas if a little advance planning and preparation is done. The rewards, I promise, are far greater than the effort needed.

Christmas Day Menus

Lunch   Salmon crowns

Roast turkey
Parsley & thyme stuffing
Bacon rolls
Chipolata sausages
Bread sauce
Cranberry sauce
Gravy
Croquette potatoes
Baked red cabbage
Buttered sprouts

Christmas pudding and brandy sauce
Mincepies

Cheeseboard - your own personal selection

Coffee and liqueurs
Chocolates

Tea   Christmas cake, Chocolate log, Sponge drops

Supper   Egg mayonnaise flavoured with fresh orange zest and
garnished with watercress

Savoury gateau
Christmas terrine
Golden chutney
Winter salad
Cucumber and onion salad

Lemon trifle
Rich chocolate creams
Coffee

Salmon crowns - serves 8

8 cooked pastry bases (5cm/2") in diameter (recipe page 53)
213gm tin red salmon
50gms (2ozs) cream cheese
1 teas.horseradish cream
a good pinch mustard powder
freshly ground white pepper
1 teas. cider or wine vinegar
2-3 slices smoked salmon
few sprigs fresh parsley
lemon slices

Drain the juice from the salmon and keep. Put the salmon, cheese, horseradish, mustard, pepper and vinegar into a food processor and process to a smooth paste. Put a tablespoon on to each pastry base and shape like a pyramid. Cut the smoked salmon into strips and wrap round the salmon paste, garnish the top with fresh parsley and a lemon slice. Serve.

Useful tips - if the salmon paste is too dry, moisten it with some of the salmon juices, if it is too soft, add a few breadcrumbs. This paste can be made and stored, covered, in a fridge. Cocktail Blini's can be used as an alternative base.

The Turkey

I know of very few cooks who do not have nightmares about roasting the turkey. December 25th is the only day we have turkey and I have notes going back some 25 years on the different methods and oven temperatures I have followed. The luxury of my 4-oven Aga does not always guarantee success because the oven temperatures cannot be instantly adjusted. Evenso I must be doing something right because the family returns each year for a repeat performance. Here are my tips on turkey roasting.

Think of the turkey as a large chicken, this will instantly alleviate all anxiety over the roasting. Begin by adding the approximate weight of a chosen stuffing to the weight of the turkey (without giblets), then work out the roasting time allowing 15mins. to each 400gms (1 lb). For example, for a turkey, (including stuffing) weighing 6kls (13lbs 8ozs) the approximate roasting time should be 3hrs. 20mins. After roasting allow the turkey to rest for 30mins before it is carved, this allows the juices which have risen during roasting to fall and keep the turkey moist.

Turkeys from Supermarkets give their own roasting instructions.

To prepare the turkey for roasting

Set oven at gas mark 7/475f/235c/Aga roasting oven.
Add the chosen stuffing to the turkey then place it on a trivet in a large roasting tin. Smear butter or oil over the skin and pour 20ozs (lpt) boiling water into the pan. Put into the pre-set oven and roast for 30 mins. Remove from the oven and cover completely with foil, return to oven and reduce the temperature to gas 4/400f/200c/Aga baking oven for the remainder of the roasting time. Remove from oven, remove foil (taking care, hot steam may escape). Test by sticking a matchstick into the thickest part of the leg, if the juices run clear the turkey is cooked, if not, return to the oven and continue roasting and testing every 10mins. The juices from the pan should be kept, pour them into a basin or similar container and when cold store them in a fridge, they provide excellent stock for soups, sauces, bakes or casseroles, remove the fat before use.

Parsley and Thyme stuffing

200gms (8ozs) bread (brown or white)
1 tbls. dried parsley
1 teas. dried thyme
freshly ground white pepper
1 size 1 egg
1 lemon - zest and juice

Break the bread into pieces and put into a food processor or liquidiser and switch on until it has crumbed. Add the parsley, thyme and pepper and process for a few seconds before adding the remaining ingredients and process until it blends together.

Useful tips - dried breadcrumbs can be used but they will need a little more liquid, (stock or water). The consistency should be "sticky" to the touch. When using both zest and juice of a lemon it is easier to remove the zest before squeezing the lemon. The stuffing should be allowed to rest for 30 mins. before it is baked. Use to stuff a turkey or chicken. It can also be shaped into balls and baked in a lightly oiled ovenproof dish, dot each with butter and bake for 20-30mins depending on the temperature of the oven. Serve hot or cold. Store, covered in a fridge. Crumble any remaining bits into a soup.

Dried breadcrumbs

Crumb bread in a food processor or liquidiser. Place on a tin tray and dry in a cool oven or on top of an Aga. Store in jars.

Bacon rolls

Set oven at gas 6/450f/220c/Aga roasting oven.

Using lean streaky or back bacon slices, remove rind and excess fat and stretch each slice by stroking with a knife, roll up and put on to a metal skewer. Place the prepared skewers over a baking tin (I use an old swiss roll tin) and bake in the pre-set oven until crisp, turning them half way through baking. Remove the rolls from the skewers and drain off all excess fat on kitchen paper before serving hot or cold.

Useful tips - cooked bacon rolls have many uses. When baked, allow them to become cold then wrap them in a parcel of greaseproof and foil and store in a fridge, use within 5 days. To serve from the fridge put the parcel into an oven until they are hot, or in a microwave without the foil cover. Bacon rolls can also be prepared as described above, and cooked under a hot grill.

Chipolata sausages

Set oven at gas 7/450f/220c/Aga roasting oven.

Pierce the skin of each sausage with a metal skewer before arranging them in a baking tin (I use a swiss roll tin). Bake until they are brown and crisp all over, drain on kitchen paper and serve.

Useful tips - These, or any cooked sausages are a most valuable ingredient to have in store. When cold, wrap the cooked sausages in a parcel of greaseproof paper and foil and store them in a fridge (use within 5 days). Serve them cold fridge or put the parcel into an oven until the sausages are hot throughout.

Bread sauce

1 medium onion - skin
10 whole cloves
1 dried bayleaf
10ozs milk
100gms (4ozs) fresh white breadcrumbs
freshly ground white pepper
several good pinches cayenne pepper
25gms (1oz) butter
1 tbls. single cream - optional

Spike the onion with the cloves and put into a small pan with the milk and bayleaf. Bring slowly to simmer, without lid, remove from heat, cover and leave for 30mins. Remove the onion and bayleaf, bring the milk to boil and stir in the fresh breadcrumbs, season with freshly ground, and cayenne pepper and simmer, without lid, until it is thick. Remove from heat and stir in the butter and cream. Serve hot with roast turkey or chicken.

Useful tips - this sauce can be made two or three days in advance. Store it, covered, in a fridge and reheat to serve. This recipe was passed on to me by my Mother-in-law who cooked the most delicious Sunday roasts, I can recommend it to you.

Cranberry sauce

200gms (8ozs) sugar
10ozs water (half pint)
250gms (10ozs) cranberries
3ozs port

Put the sugar and water into a large pan and stir over a gentle heat until the sugar has dissolved. Add the cranberries and port, and boil, without lid on pan, for 10mins. Remove from heat and cool a little before pouring into clean hot jars. Cover with a disc of paper and seal with a lid. When cold label and store in a cool dry place.

Useful tips - home-made cranberry sauce is perfect served with turkey. It also makes an acceptable gift. A valuable ingredient to have in store, it can be added to many recipes giving additional colour and flavour.

Croquette potatoes

Set oven at gas 4/400f/200c/Aga baking oven.

Mash boiled potatoes with butter and milk and season with freshly grated nutmeg. Shape into sausage shapes approximately 5cms (2") in length. Coat in beaten egg then fresh or dried breadcrumbs (recipe on page 25). Place on a lightly oiled baking tin or tray and bake for 20-30mins. or until hot. Serve with the Christmas day turkey.

Useful tips - make in advance and store on a baking sheet covered with greaseproof and foil, in a fridge until needed - serve within 5 days. I do not recommend freezing.

Gravy - made from turkey giblet stock

Soak the turkey giblets in a pan of salted water for about an hour, strain and cover with fresh water, bring to a simmer, uncovered. Skim the top, cover and simmer for 1-2hrs over a gentle heat or in the simmering oven of an Aga. Remove the giblets from the pan. Mix approximately 50gms (2ozs) plain flour with a little cold water, stir this into the pan juices adding a few spots of gravy browning and 5ozs red wine, stir and boil, without lid, for about 2mins. or until the gravy begins to thicken. Remove from heat and allow to become cold. To serve, remove any fat which has formed on the top, bring back to a boil then reduce to a simmer for a few minutes, serve. If you have the luxury of an Aga this final simmering can be done in the simmering oven.

Useful tips - I make the gravy as soon as I have the turkey giblets. When cold store in a fridge or cold larder. Any gravy remaining after Christmas Day can be added to a soup.

Baked red cabbage

Set oven at gas 6/450f/220c/Aga roasting oven.

Slice a whole red cabbage and put into an ovenproof casserole, add 1 tbls. demerera sugar, 2 tbls. cider or wine vinegar and 4tbls. water, stir, put lid on casserole and bake in the pre-heated oven for 10mins. then lower temperature to gas 3/150f/75c/Aga simmering oven and continue baking for 1 hr. Serve straight from the oven or, when cold, store in a fridge and reheat for serving.

Useful tips - I serve baked red cabbage with our Christmas lunch. It is a very useful winter vegetable. I cook a whole large cabbage and reheat as and when I need it, either on top or in the oven.

Buttered sprouts

Remove all damaged outer leaves from the sprouts before washing. Add to boiling water and boil, with lid on pan, until cooked to your liking. Strain off the water, add a nut of butter to the pan and return to a gentle heat and dry off the cooked sprouts in the butter. Serve.

The Christmas Pudding

The following is a very old Smith family recipe. Although it might be questioned whether making Christmas puddings should come under the heading of "Lazy Cook", I think of it as part of the Christmas preparation not to be missed. I make them when the family is around and we can all stir and wish. I make an extra large one for our family Christmas Day lunch in the hope there will be some remaining for a Boxing Day pudding. I also make very small ones to give as presents, especially to friends living alone.

Christmas pudding - makes 3 x 1kg (21b) puddings

300gms (12ozs) raisins
300gms (12ozs) sultanas
300gms (12ozs) currants
200gms (8ozs) dark cane sugar
150gms (6ozs) mixed peel
150gms (6ozs) fresh breadcrumbs (brown or white)
300gms (12ozs) grated suet
150gms (6ozs) plain flour
1 teas. mixed spice
300gms (12ozs) grated cooking apple
50gms (2ozs) flaked almonds - browned
1 small carrot - grated
Zest of 1 lemon
5 size 1 eggs - whisk
3ozs brandy
50gms (2ozs) butter
100gms (4ozs) whole almonds with skins

Butter each basin spreading it thickly over the base and into this press the whole almonds. Mix all remaining ingredients together and pack into the prepared basins. Cover with buttered greaseproof paper then foil (each pleated in the middle), and tie with string. Steam for 6-8hrs or until the puddings are dark and firm to the touch. Allow to cool before storing in a cool, dry place. Reheat in oven to serve.

Useful tips - one of the things that puts people off making Christmas puddings is a kitchen full of steam. This can be avoided by steaming them in the oven. Stand the basins in a large roasting tin, pour in a kettle of boiling water, cover with foil, put into oven (gas 3/150f/100c/Aga simmering oven) for 6-8hrs or until cooked. Add more boiling water as necessasry but unlike traditional steaming, it is no disaster if the pan runs dry. I put them in the oven overnight. Put the pudding in the oven or in a microwave to reheat before serving. If I am really organised I make the puddings a year in advance, usually in January. Remove them from the basins when cooked and wrap them in greaseproof and foil, store in a tin in a cool dry place, or freeze.

Brandy sauce
20ozs (1pt) milk
2 desst. cornflour
1 desst. sugar
brandy - a liberal amount

Mix a little of the milk and the cornflour to a smooth paste. Put the remaining milk into a pan and heat, stir in the cornflour paste and brandy and stir until it boils. Remove from heat, add sugar to taste and serve.

Useful tips - this can be made in advance and reheated for serving. To store pour into a basin and cover with cling film. Reheat in an Aga oven or microwave, cling film removed. I always serve brandy sauce with the Christmas pudding on Christmas Day as my Mother did.

Mincepies
These can be made from shortcrust, wholemeal or puff pastry, home-made or bought, (see recipe for home-made pastry page 53). I make some from shortcrust and some from wholemeal pastry. I also make some very small

ones using a 3cm (1 ") cutter and bake them on baking sheets rather then in patti tins, this smaller size is useful to serve after a meal or at a drinks party. Store mincepies in airtight tins, they will keep for months.

Mincemeat - makes approx. 7 lbs

400gms (1 lb) raisins
200gms (8ozs) sultanas
300gms (12ozs) currants
100gms (4ozs) split almonds
3 large cooking apples - peel, core and chop roughly
200gms (8ozs) chopped mixed peel
200gms (8ozs) shredded suet
150gms (6ozs) dark cane or demerara sugar
2 lemons - juice and zest
half teasp. cinnamon powder
half teasp. mixed spice
10ozs brandy

Process the raisins, sultanas, currants, almonds and cooking apples until they are well chopped, then mix with the remaining ingredients. Pack into jars, top with a greaseproof disc and a lid and store in a cool, dark place.

Useful tips - it is necessary to process the fruit to release the juices. Beef or vegetarian suet can be used. I pack into jars of varying sizes. Make 2 months before it is needed. If you can remember, turn the jars during the storing time. Stir well before using, if the consistency is too dry, stir in more brandy or fresh orange juice. Home-made mincemeat has a good flavour and is not syrupy-sweet.

Fudge

410gm tin evaporated milk
50gms (2ozs) butter
400gms (1 lb) granulated sugar

Butter a shallow tin approximately 20cms (8") square. Melt the butter in the milk in a large heavy-based pan. Add the sugar and stir over a low heat until it has all dissolved. Turn up the heat until it boils and rises in the pan, taking care from this point that it does not boil over. When the mixture reduces in quantity and turns a darker colour remove from heat and test by dropping a few spots from a wooden spatula or spoon, into a glass of cold water. If the fudge remains in one solid piece it has reached setting point, if it disintegrates into the water it needs further boiling. When setting point is reached, add the chosen flavouring and pour into the prepared tin. Allow to cool before cutting into squares. Store in a box.

Additional flavours - add after setting point is reached
1)   1 teaspoon vanilla essence.
2)   half teas. ground ginger and 100gms (4ozs) chopped crystalised ginger.
3)   100gms (4ozs) bitter melted chocolate
4)   100gms (4ozs) bitter melted chocolate and 25gms (1oz) browned, flaked almonds.
5)   100gms (4ozs) chopped walnuts and orange zest

Useful tips - the fudge must boil quite rapidly before it will reach setting point, it should only need an occasional stir during this boiling. Take great care that it does not boil over, I try not to leave the kitchen for a length of time when making fudge

Chocolate peppermint creams
400gms (1 lb) icing sugar
1 egg white
1 tbls. water
1 teas. peppermint essence (or a few spots peppermint oil)
green colouring
100gms (4ozs) bitter chocolate

Put the icing sugar into a food processor and process for a few seconds. Lightly whisk the egg white with water, a spot of green colour and the peppermint essence and pour on to the icing sugar with the machine switched on until it forms a ball. Remove from processor and work to a pliable paste with more sieved icing sugar, roll to 5mm (quarter inch) thickness and cut with a 3cm (1") plain cutter. Place on foil or greaseproof lightly sifted with icing sugar, to dry. Melt the chocolate and dip half of each peppermint cream in this. Place on clean foil and when set store in a box.

Useful tips - avoid adding too much colouring by dropping it from a skewer. For ease of rolling, take small quantities from the processor at a time, cover the remainder with a damp cloth or kitchen roll. On Valentine's day shape with a heart cutter and cover completely in chocolate. To use less chocolate, trail melted chocolate from a spoon in lines over the peppermint creams.

Almond chocolates (1) - makes 24-30
125gms (4ozs) ground almonds
125gms (4ozs) caster sugar
125gms (4ozs) icing sugar
1 teas. fresh lemon juice
1-2 tbls. brandy
a few spots vanilla essence
a few spots almond essence
250gms (8ozs) bitter chocolate
125gms (4ozs) whole almonds - with skins

Mix the ground almonds, caster and icing sugars together in a basin. Mix the lemon juice, brandy and essences together and mix into the dry ingredients with a fork to make a paste. Using a little icing sugar shape into rounds and flatten with thumb. Melt the chocolate slowly in the oven or a microwave and coat each round in chocolate. Remove with a fork on to foil, press a whole almond on top and leave to set. Store in a box and put into a chocolate case to serve.

Useful tips - chocolate is not the easiest ingredient with which to work and when making chocolates the aim is to keep the chocolate shiny. To achieve this, melt two-thirds of the chocolate, grate the remainder and stir this into the melted chocolate until it becomes smooth. Always avoid steam or water coming into contact with melted chocolate for coating. Always use the best bitter chocolate with a high percentage of cocoa solids. A few home-made chocolates in a bag or box make a very acceptable present.

Almond chocolates (2) - makes approx 60
250gms (10ozs) ground almonds
200gms (8ozs) icing sugar
200gms (8ozs) caster sugar
25gms (1oz) cocoa powder
1 small egg
1 tbls. lemon juice
2 tbls. chocolate liqueur (Creme de cacao)
300gms (12ozs) white chocolate for coating

Mix the dry ingredients together, whisk the egg, lemon juice and liqueur, add to dry ingredients and work to a paste. Shape into rounds and allow to dry before coating in melted white chocolate. Place on foil to harden. Store in a box.

Hazelnut chocolates - makes approx. 30
400gms (1 lb) bitter chocolate
100gms (4ozs) butter
200gms (8ozs) ground hazelnuts
100gms (4ozs) whole hazelnuts

Melt 200gm/6ozs of the chocolate with the butter and mix to a cream, stir in enough ground hazelnuts to make a stiff paste. Shape into batons approx. 3cms/1" in length and leave to dry on foil. Brown the whole hazelnuts in a hot oven or under a grill, then rub off the skins. Melt the remaining chocolate and coat each baton in this, place on foil, put a whole hazelnut in the centre and when set hard store in a box.

White chocolate ginger tablets - approx 30
200gms (8ozs) white chocolate
1 small level teaspoon ground ginger
150gms (6ozs) crystalised ginger - chopped

Melt the chocolate, stir in the ginger then drop from a teaspoon on to foil, shape into discs and put chopped ginger on top. When hard store in a box.

Christmas cake - to fit a 24cm (10") round tin
250gms (10ozs) butter - softened
200gms (8ozs) dark cane or muscavado sugar
1 tbls. molasses
6 size 1 eggs
350gms (14ozs) plain flour
1 teas. mixed spice
400gms (1 lb) currants
250gms (10ozs) sultanas
250gms (10ozs) raisins
150gms (6ozs) mixed chopped peel
100gms (4ozs) glace cherries - leave whole
100gms (4ozs) flaked almonds - browned, crush in hand
Brandy - to be added after baking

Set oven at gas 3/300f/150c/Aga simmering oven.
Line the base and sides of the cake tin with greaseproof (no need to grease).
Cream the butter and sugar together, add the eggs, molasses, flour and spice
and mix to a smooth soft consistency. Mix all the remaining ingredients
together (not the brandy) and stir into the butter mixture. Pack into
prepared tin, level the top. Stand on a baking sheet and bake in the pre-set
oven for 6-8hrs or until set, (test by putting a metal skewer into the centre, if
it comes out clean the cake is baked). Remove from oven and allow to cool a
little before turning on to a wire tray. When cold prick all over the top with a
metal skewer and pour a liberal amount of brandy into the cake. Wrap in
greaseproof and foil and store in a cool, dry place until required for decoration.

Useful tips - oven temperatures vary so much and I recommend you look at
the cake after 4hrs. A second indication of the cake being baked is when
cracks appear around the edge. I was given this recipe many years ago by an
Aunt and I use it for all Christmas, wedding or special occasion cakes, it is
rich and moist. Pour more brandy into the cake before decorating. Bake
two or three months before serving, it will improve on keeping.

Chocolate log

Fatless sponge -
2 size 1 eggs
50gms (2 ozs) caster sugar
50gms (2 ozs) plain flour
1 teas. cocoa powder

Chocolate buttercream for filling and covering -
150gms (6ozs) icing sugar
1 tbls. drinking chocolate
150gms (6ozs) butter - softened
a little milk or single cream
a sprig of holly for decoration

To make the sponge -
Set oven at gas 4/400f/200c/Aga baking oven.
Put the eggs and sugar into a mixer bowl and place in the oven, with the whisk or beaters, to warm (this should take approx. 5mins.) Line a Swiss roll tin with greaseproof, lightly oiled. Sieve the flour and cocoa powder together. Take the bowl from the oven and whisk at full speed until the mixture is thick, sieve in the flour and cocoa and stir until smooth. Pour into the prepared tin and bake for 15-20mins. or until set, turn on to a piece of greaseproof paper and peel off the greaseproof in which it has baked, roll in the new greaseproof and leave to become cold. To make the chocolate butter cream process the icing sugar and drinking chocolate for a few seconds add the butter and process until smooth, soften to a spreadable consistency with a little milk or single cream. Unroll the sponge and spread with half the butter cream, roll and place on a serving dish before covering it all over with the remaining butter cream. Mark it with a fork to represent the bark of a tree, and decorate with holly, or a suitable Christmas decoration.

Useful tips - my idea of warming the eggs and sugar speeds up the thickening process considerably (this can be done in the simmering oven of an Aga). Do not use plastic bowl or whisk. Watch carefully, the eggs must not cook. This recipe can be made and frozen, thaw thoroughly before serving.

Sponge drops - makes approx. 30

Set oven at gas 6/450f/220c/Aga roasting oven.

Follow the directions for mixing a fatless sponge described in the chocolate log recipe (page 35), omitting the cocoa powder. Lightly oil a large baking sheet, or cover with bake-o-glide. Drop dessertspoons of the mixture on to the prepared baking sheet and shape into rounds, sprinkle with caster sugar and bake until they become a pale biscuit colour (4-8mins). Remove from oven and remove immediately from the baking sheet on to wire trays. When cold store in an airtight tin.

Useful tips - these will store well and are very useful to have in store. They are light and delicious and can be served in the following ways - as a biscuit, with fruit compotes or creams, or sandwiched together with fresh cream and strawberry jam. They can be piped, through a plain nozzle, into fingers. Because of their lightness they are good to take to friends who are unwell or in hospital.

Supper

Egg mayonnaise flavoured with fresh orange zest and garnished with watercress

1 egg per person - hard boiled
Mayonnaise - recipe on page 37
orange zest
watercress

Shell the eggs and cut in half, place on individual serving plates, cut side down, and coat with mayonnaise. Put a little orange zest on the top and surround with sliced watercress.

Useful tips - the eggs can be hard boiled and stored in a fridge, use within 3 days. If the mayonnaise is too thick to coat the eggs, thin it down by stirring in a little fresh orange juice. Serve individually, or on one large serving dish.

Mayonnaise - made in a food processor or liquidiser

1 size 1 egg
1 desst. cider or wine vinegar
half a teaspoon sugar
half a teaspoon mustard powder
half a teaspoon ground white pepper
half a teaspoon salt
10ozs (approximately) oil

Put all the ingredients except the oil into a food processor or liquidiser and process for a few seconds then, with the machine still running, gradually add the oil until the mayonnaise thickens to the required consistency. Put into a jar with a lid and store in fridge.

Useful tip - I make mayonnaise with sunflower oil but a mixture of oils can be used. If the mayonnaise is too thick thin it down by stirring in a little warm water or fruit juice. It is another very useful ingredient to have in store especially at party time.

Savoury gateau - serves 8-10 slices

1 x 400gms (1 lb) loaf - brown or white, tin or cob shape
50gms (2ozs) butter or margarine - softened
150gms (6ozs) meat paté
150gms (6ozs) fish paté
200gms (8ozs) cream or curd cheese
a little single cream or milk
freshly ground white pepper
100gms (4ozs) chopped walnuts
apple slices, grapes, radish, lemon or orange slices - for garnish

Remove all the crusts from the loaf before slicing it horizontally into 3 slices of equal thickness. Spread each slice with butter and sandwich together with the paté so that it looks like one big sandwich, place it on a serving dish. Soften the cheese with a little cream or milk and season with freshly ground white pepper and cover the loaf with this. Press the chopped walnuts into the cheese and garnish the top with the suggested ingredients. Slice to serve.

Useful tips - this is an excellent recipe to make and freeze so that it is ready to garnish and serve over the Christmas and New Year holiday. It makes a refreshing change from poultry, meat or game you may have enjoyed over Christmas. Assemble it to the "big sandwich" stage and freeze until needed. Make sure it has completely thawed before the cream cheese and garnish are added. Many different fillings can be used. Home-made patés make a very delicious gateau but if time is at a premium buy good quality ones. It is a most attractive recipe to serve and popular with vegetarians.

Christmas terrine - serves 8-10
2 chicken breasts
300gms (12ozs) pork
300gms (12ozs) venison or gamey sausages
175gms (7ozs) packet diced bacon lardons
2 teas dried herbes de Provence
several good pinches ground mace
freshly ground black pepper
2ozs port
50gms (2ozs) pistachio nuts - shell and halve
dried bayleaves
home made stock - recipe on page 49

Cut the chicken and pork into mouthsized pieces, skin the sausages. Mix all ingredients (except the stock) together with a fork and leave to marinade for 2hrs. Stir well before packing into a terrine dish/s. Press a dried bayleaf into the top, cover with a lid and bake in a bain marie for 1hr - oven temperature gas 3/300f/150c/Aga simmering oven. Remove from baking tin, place a heavy weight on top and pour in stock or savoury jelly. When cold remove weight and store the terrine, covered, in a fridge. Bring back to room temperature to serve.

Useful tips - bake in a bain marie (a water bath), as follows - stand the terrine in a roasting tin or ovenproof dish and pour hand-hot water to come half way up the dish. If home made stock is not available, using gellatine crystals, make up a savoury jelly following the instructions given on the packet.

Golden Chutney - makes 5-6 lbs

200gms (8ozs) dried apricots
100gms (4ozs) cranberries
200gms (8ozs) dates - cut up
200gms (8ozs) dried prunes - cut up
200gms (8ozs) crystalised or preserved ginger cut into pieces
200gms (8ozs) sultanas
400gms (1 lb) dark brown sugar
850ml (30ozs) spiced vinegar

Put all ingredients into a preserving or large pan and stir over a gentle heat until the sugar has completely dissolved. Bring to a simmer and simmer until most of the liquid has evaporated and the chutney has thickened, without lid on pan. Allow to cool a little before pouring into hot jars. Cover with a disc of paper and seal with a plastic lid. Label and store in a cool dry place.

Useful tips - If fresh cranberries are not available use frozen or dried. I first made this chutney to use up all the fruit and bits left over from Christmas but it has proved so popular that I am rarely without it. Serve it with cold meats or cheese or add a tablespoon to a pasta or rice dish, a soup, sauce or casserole, it will make a marvellous difference to the flavour. Pot it into jars of various sizes and give one as a present at Christmas, your friends will love it and will want the recipe. It takes approximately one hour to prepare, cook and pot - very " Lazy Cook".

Winter salad

Watercress, celery, spring onions, carrot, radish, Chinese leaves, a selection of nuts, crumbled cheese, grated parsnip - chop or slice where necessary and mix all together. Dress with oil and vinegar to serve.

Cucumber and onion salad

Peel and slice one whole cucumber and mix with one large sweet onion, skinned and finely sliced. Cover with oil and vinegar, (two-thirds oil, one third cider or wine vinegar), serve within a day of making. To me cucumber is a summer salad ingredient but my Mother always served this salad with cold meats over the Christmas holiday and for that reason I always make it continuing one of many family Christmas traditions.

Lemon trifle - serves 6
1 pkt trifle sponges
lemon curd
3 lemons - juice and zest
icing sugar (approx 50gms/2ozs)
5ozs double cream - whipped

Split the trifle sponges and spread each half with lemon curd, place them in a serving dish. Remove the zest from each lemon and keep. Squeeze the juice from two and a half lemons and pour over the trifle sponges, mash with a fork. Using the juice from the remaining half lemon make up a runny icing and pour this over the sponge mixture, cover with cling film and leave for 1-24 hours. To serve top with whipped cream and scatter with the lemon zest.

Useful tips - this trifle is more delicious the longer the sponges soak in the lemon juice, make it a day in advance of serving if possible and add the cream and zest to serve. It is an ideal sweet to serve following all the rich Christmas fayre. Make it in a shallow dish rather than the traditional deep trifle dish.

Rich chocolate creams - makes 6
1 teas. instant coffee granuals
1 teas. cocoa powder
100gms (4ozs) bitter chocolate
10ozs whipping cream
200gms (8ozs) cream or curd cheese
2 tbls. chocolate liqueur
50gms (2ozs) split almonds - slightly browned

Dissolve the coffee and cocoa powder in a tablespoon of boiling water. Melt the chocolate. Put all ingredients, except the almonds, into a food processor and process until a smooth, soft consistency. Put into 6 small glasses or ramekins, cover with cling film and store in a fridge. To serve, bring back to room temperature, crush the almonds and place on top.

Useful tips - make this recipe two or three days before serving to allow the flavours to blend. It is very rich so choose small serving dishes. An alternative presentation is to pipe the mixture into the dishes and top with a chocolate square or chocolate lace.

Chocolate squares

Spread melted chocolate on to a piece of foil and allow to set before cutting into squares. Make in advance and store in a box.

Chocolate lace

Pipe melted chocolate on to foil in lacey shapes. Store on the foil, in a box, peel off to use.

Boxing Day

Boxing day starts late and is mostly taken up with a long walk with friends and neighbours. Towards the end of the walk thoughts turn to ginger wine and something nice to eat. The menu I suggest is intended to give the cook another day out of the kitchen. The meal can be prepared by anyone who can handle a knife, a chopping board and a saucepan and who happens to be first up!

Menu for a meal after a walk

Ginger wine

Turkey and mushroom bake
Savoury rice

Boxing day pudding
Coffee meringue gateau

Cheeseboard

Coffee

Selection of home-made fudge

Ginger Wine

I was introduced to this shortly after coming to Bisley. Eileen Worsley, a friend and neighbour, invited me to help to decorate the church with poppies for the Remembrance Day service. After a morning in a cold church we would return to her homely kitchen and drink ginger wine - it's so wonderfully warming and comforting on a cold winter day.

Turkey and mushroom bake - serves 8-10

800gms (2lbs) cooked turkey - broken into mouthsized pieces
50gms (2ozs) butter
10ozs milk
2 teas. mushroom ketchup
freshly ground black pepper
400gms (1 lb) mushrooms - wipe and slice
50gms (2 ozs) plain flour
20 ozs stock

Set oven to gas mark 6/450f/220c/Aga roasting oven. Put the turkey into an ovenproof dish. Melt the butter in a large pan with the milk. Add the mushroom ketchup, pepper and sliced mushrooms, stir and simmer until the mushrooms have softened. Mix the flour to a smooth paste with cold water and stir into the mushroom mixture with the stock. Stir until boiling then simmer until it thickens, add more stock if the sauce is too thick, (it should be the consistency of thick gravy). Pour over the turkey and bake, covered, until hot and bubbling.

Useful tips - The juices from the turkey can be added to this sauce (see page 24) This recipe can be prepared in advance of serving, cover and store in a fridge. Cooked sausages or ham can also be added with the turkey.

Savoury rice

Stir cooked peas, sweetcorn and herbs into cooked rice with a few good pinchs curry powder and a little single cream. Serve hot or cold.

Boxing day pudding

Cold Christmas pudding
brandy
15ozs milk
1 teas.vanilla essence
3 size 1 eggs

Set oven at gas 3/300f/150c/Aga simmering oven.
Slice the pudding into an ovenproof dish and sprinkle liberally with brandy.
Warm the milk and vanilla essence, whisk the eggs and sieve into the milk, stir then pour over the pudding slices and bake, uncovered, until set. Serve from the oven with single cream.

Useful tips - this is an excellent way of using up leftover Christmas pudding. It can be quickly prepared ahead of baking. It is a very rich and delicious pudding and our Christmas menus would be incomplete without it.

Coffee meringue gateau - serves 8-10

2 meringue plates - recipe page 45
2 teas. instant coffee granuals
10ozs double cream
5ozs thick single cream
50gms (2ozs) bitter chocolate - grated

Dissolve the coffee granuals in a tablespoon of boiling water, cool a little then add to the creams and whip until it is a soft, spreadable consistency. Sandwich the meringue plates together using half the cream and spread the remainder on top, scatter with grated chocolate.

Useful tips - this pudding should be made several hours before it is to be served, the longer it is left the better the flavour. Store before serving in a fridge or cold larder. As with all meringue puddings, it is very popular.

Meringue plates - to make 2 x 25cms (10")

4 size 1 egg whites
200gms (8ozs) caster sugar
pinch cream of tartare

Set oven at gas 2/200f/100c/Aga simmering oven.
Cover 2 baking sheets with household parchment or bake-o-glide. Whisk the egg whites until they are stiff and dry (of a cottonwool texture). Whisk or fold in the sugar and cream of tartare and spread the mixture equally on to the prepared baking sheets in rounds approximately 25cms/10" in diameter. Place in pre-set oven to dry (this can take between 2 and 4 hours). Take from oven and remove from paper, store in airtight polythene or freezer bags until needed.

Useful tips - make sure the whites are really stiff before the sugar is added. They are dry when then can be peeled from the paper. A most useful ingredient to have in store, they will remain crisp for at least 2 months.

Let's have a party

Christmas is party time and one of the easiest ways I know of entertaining lots of people is to give a 'Soup and Mince pie' party. Although the preparation is minimal everyone leaves feeling well satisfied, if not replete. 'Soup and Mince pie' parties are a very easy and enjoyable way to 'fund raise'.

Party Menu

Hot Punch
Savoury Choux

Turkey soup
Tangy tomato soup
Selection of breads and rolls

Mincepies and mince tarts

Cheeseboard - of your own personal choice
Fresh fruit - seasonal selection

Coffee
Home-made vanilla fudge

Hot punch - approx. 20 glasses
1 bottle inexpensive red wine
half a bottle ruby port
20ozs (1pt) strong China tea
10ozs (half pint) ginger ale
freshly grated nutmeg
1 cinnamon stick
sugar to taste

Put all ingredients into a large saucepan and bring slowly to simmer.

Useful tips - make a few hours before needed to allow all the flavours to blend, reheat to serve.

Savoury choux - to make 40-50 cocktail size
choux pastry - made from recipe on page 48

Filling -
400gms (1 lb) cream cheese
chopped parsley - fresh if possible otherwise dried
freshly ground white pepper
2 teas. Dijon mustard
a little single cream or milk

Set oven at gas 7/450f/220c/Aga roasting oven.
Drop small teaspoons of the choux pastry on to a large, lightly oiled baking sheet and bake in the pre-set oven for 15-20mins. or until crisp and golden. Remove from oven and, using a pointed knife make a slit in each to allow steam to escape, cool on a wire tray. To serve, flavour the cheese with the listed ingredients and soften, if necessary, with a little cream or milk. Fill the baked choux cases with the cheese and serve, piled on to a dish.

Useful tips - I find these are really popular at parties. They can quickly be baked on the day or frozen in time for the event. Follow instructions in main choux pastry recipe for serving from the freezer.

Choux pastry

5 ozs cold water
50gms (2ozs) butter
75gms (3ozs) plain flour
2 size 1 eggs

Set oven at gas 7/450f/220c/Aga roasting oven.
Put the water and butter into a pan and heat slowly until the butter has melted, increase the heat and when the liquid begins to rise in the pan add the flour and beat until the mixture leaves the side of the pan, remove from heat and leave to cool a little before adding the eggs and beating until the mixture is smooth. Bake as directed in the recipe of your choice.

Useful tips - always bake choux pastry in a hot oven. It should be crisp and light in texture. It can be served with savoury or sweet fillings and is best eaten the day it is baked, otherwise I recommend freezing. To serve from the freezer thaw the baked choux then place in a hot oven for a few minutes to crisp. Once made the mixture can be kept for several hours before it is baked. I think choux is one of the easiest pastries to make. It can be used to create the most exciting sweet and savoury "Lazy Cook" creations.

Turkey soup - 8-10 servings

1 large onion - skin and chop
1 large carrot - thinly sliced
1 pkt bacon lardons
200gms (8ozs) dark mushrooms - wipe and chop
1 teas. mushroom ketchup
200-400gms (8ozs-1 lb) cooked turkey - broken into small pieces
1 ltr (2pts) turkey stock - see recipe on page 49
juices remaining from the turkey roasting if still available
freshly ground black pepper
1 teas. dried mixed herbs

Cover the base of a large pan with cold water, bring to boil and add the onion and carrot, put lid on pan and cook until the onion has softened. Add the lardons and when cooked add all remaining ingredients, stir, bring to simmer. Skim the top, put lid on pan and simmer for 30mins to 1 hour. Serve hot with bread or rolls.

Useful tips - this soup can be thickened with fresh breadcrumbs or with flour - mix a tablespoon plain flour with cold water and stir it into the cooked soup, boil for 2mins. Chicken or game soup can be made using this recipe. I prefer to make it and store it in a fridge for 2 or 3 days before serving.

Tangy tomato soup - serves 6-8

1 large onion - skin and finely chop
2 carrots - wash and slice thinly
800gms tin tomatoes
1 ltr (30ozs) stock - ham, chicken, vegetable (or a mixture)
2 tbls. orange marmalade
freshly ground white pepper
half teas. mixed dried herbs

Soften the onion and carrots in a little boiling water with lid on pan then process or liquidise with the tomatoes, return to pan, add the stock, marmalade, pepper and herbs and simmer with lid on pan for 30mins. Serve topped with orange zest and/or a swirl of cream. Store, covered, in a fridge, use within 5 days.

Useful tips - recipes for stocks can be found on pages 49/50.
This is one of the quickest and most popular soups I make - very "Lazy Cook" and very good. Make well in advance and freeze in freezer bags.

Stock making - the" Lazy Cook" way

There is something very wholesome and satisfying about adding a little jellied stock to a recipe. My method of making stock, though not traditional, gives good quick results and a stock superior to any which can be bought.

Meat

Put bones/carcass, cooked or uncooked, into a pan, cover with cold water, bring slowly to boil, without lid~ skim the top, place lid on pan, and simmer for 1-2hrs (this can be done in the simmering oven of an Aga). Strain into a basin and when cold store in a fridge (use within 2 days), or remove the fat which will have set on the surface, and freeze the stock until required. For convenience of use I freeze stock in bags of varying sizes.

Fish

Put uncooked fish bones, skin, heads into a pan and cover with cold water. Bring slowly to boil, without lid, skim the top, add 8-10 peppercorns and a bayleaf1 place lid on top and simmer for 20mins. Strain into a basin and follow directions for storing as for meat stock.

Vegetable

I don't actually make this but I strain all liquid from cooked vegetables into a jug, when cold, cover and store in a fridge, use within 2 days.

Ham

Refer to page 18.

Mincetarts

For larger parties of the" soup and mincepies" variety, I make mincetarts - put mincemeat into a ready baked flan case, cover with dried breadcrumbs, or apple slices, and heat in a hot oven.

Mincepies

Recipe on page 29.

Home made Vanilla Fudge

Recipe on page 30.

New Year's Eve Dinner Party

I always look forward to our New Year's Eve dinner party. There are usually between eight and ten of us and at the end of the meal, which is often around 11.30p.m., we all don our outdoor clothes and walk across the road to church in time to hear the bells 'ring-in' the New Year. We take mince pies and Christmas cake for the ringers. Hearing a single bell striking midnight in a church on New Year's eve is a most poignant moment - a wonderful place to be.

The Lychgate, Bisley

New Year's Eve Menu

I usually plan to serve something different from the meals we have enjoyed since Christmas Day. The menu I give here is very special because it is one I served for our New Year's Eve dinner party as we entered this present millennium.

Champagne
Canapes

Cream of chestnut soup
Bread rolls

Roast baby peppers filled with rice, sundried tomatoes and prawns, served with a garlic cream sauce

Venison sausages with aubergine and bacon cooked in an apple and cranberry sauce
Baked red cabbage -
Curly cabbage
Duchesse potatoes

Lemon Sorbet

Sparkling Dome
Fresh oranges in brandy
Cheeseboard - a selection of your own choosing

Coffee and liqueurs
White chocolate ginger tablets

Cocktail canapés on pastry bases

Pastry bases (for party use) - makes 90-100
100gms (4ozs) plain white flour
100gms (4ozs) wholemeal flour
100gms (4ozs) lard
2-3ozs cold water

Set oven at gas 6/450f/220c/Aga roasting oven.
Put the flours into a food processor and process for a few seconds. Add
the lard in pieces, switch on processor and pour the liquid through the funnel
until a ball of pastry is formed. Switch off. Roll the pastry on a lightly floured
board to approximately 4mm (quarter of an inch) in thickness and cut
into rounds using a cutter 25mms (1") in diameter. Place on baking sheets,
prick lightly with a fork and bake for 10-15mins. or until they colour slightly.
Use hot or cold. Store in an airtight container, use within 1 month, or freeze.

Useful tips - these little bases are a wonderful asset at Christmas or any
party time, make them in various sizes from wholemeal or shortcrust pastry.
Top them with paté and they provide more-ish canapés. Garnish a meat
paté with a seedless grape, a fish paté with a shelled prawn, a vegetarian paté
with a sprig of parsley. They can also be shaped from leftover bits of pastry
when making mincepies or a pie topping.

Chicken liver paté

50gms (2ozs) butter
1 shallot or small onion - skin and finely chop
200gms (8ozs) chicken livers
2 tbls brandy
1 dried bayleaf
2 good pinches herbes de Provence
freshly ground white pepper
extra butter for sealing
Soften the shallot or onion in half- the butter. Add the remaining butter
and when melted add the chicken livers and cook for approximately 2mins.
turning them halfway through cooking, remove from pan. Scrape any bits
from the base of the pan, add the brandy and boil for a few seconds, remove
from heat and allow to cool slightly before putting into a processor or liquidiser

with the cooked livers and onion, process until smooth. Pack into a pot. Melt approximately 50gms/2ozs butter and pour over the paté to form a seal, when set store in a fridge. Allow to come back to room temperature before serving.

Mackerel Paté
125gms (5oz) tin mackerel fillets in olive oil
4 teas. horseradish cream
1 teas. Dijon mustard
1 tbls. breadcrumbs
freshly ground white pepper

Put all ingredients into a food processor or liquidiser and process until smooth. Put into a covered container and store in a fridge until required. Bring to room temperature before serving.

Egg paste
8-12 egg yolks - baked (see useful tips below)
1 tbls. mayonnaise
1 teas. horseradish cream
half teas. tomato purée
freshly ground white pepper

Mix all ingredients to a smooth paste in a food processor or liquidiser. Store in a fridge in a covered container, use within 3 days.

Useful tips - this is an excellent way of using up egg yolks after making meringues. To cook, put them into a buttered, ovenproof basin and bake until hard in a moderate oven - gas 3/300f/150c/Aga simmering oven.

Cheese savouries to serve with drinks - to make approx. 40
50gms (2ozs) breadcrumbs - fresh or dried
1 tbls. freshly chopped parsley (or 1 teas. dried)
1 tbls. onion - finely chopped
200gms (8ozs) Stilton cheese - crumbled
50gms (2ozs) butter - softened
1 tbls. brandy
1 teas. Lea & Perrins sauce
freshly ground pepper

Mix half the breadcrumbs with all the parsley. Put all remaining ingredients into a food processor and process together. Take teaspoonsful and coat in the breadcrumb and parsley mix. Serve immediately or store, in a covered container, in the fridge. Bring back to room temperature to serve.

Useful tips - Stilton or any blue cheese can be used, or a mixture - a good recipe for using up all the leftover bits.

Cream of chestnut soup - 6-8 servings
250gms (10ozs) dried chestnuts - soak overnight in cold water
250gms (10ozs) fresh mushrooms
10ozs (half pint) single cream
freshly ground white pepper

Put the soaked chestnuts into a large pan and cover with approximately 20ozs (1pt) fresh cold water. Bring to a simmer, put lid on pan and simmer until the chestnuts have softened. Wipe the mushrooms with damp kitchen paper, slice and add to the chestnuts, simmer for a further 10mins (with lid on pan). Using a slotted spoon remove the chestnuts and mushrooms from the pan and liquidise or process. Return to the pan of cooking liquid, stir in the cream, season with freshly ground white pepper and bring to a simmer before serving, or store, covered, in a fridge, use within 5 days.

Useful tips - I prefer to make this soup a little in advance of serving and store it, in a covered container, in a fridge. This " resting" time allows the flavours to blend resulting in a more tasty soup. Stir in the cream and bring to simmer, serve.

Roasted baby red Peppers filled with rice, sundried tomatoes and prawns, served with a garlic cream sauce - to serve 4

4 baby red peppers
2 tbls. cooked rice - brown or white
4 sundried tomatoes in oil
50gms (2ozs) cooked prawns
1 pkt. Boursin garlic cream cheese
a little single cream or milk

Set oven at gas 6/450f/220c/Aga roasting oven.
Slice the top from each pepper and remove the seeds. Cut the sundried tomatoes and mix into the rice with the prawns and a little oil, pack into the peppers and top with the lids. Lightly oil a suitable ovenproof dish, oil the peppers and lids, place in the dish and bake, uncovered, for 20-30mins. or until the peppers soften and begin to turn brown. Make the sauce by putting the Boursin and cream into a pan and whisk or stir over a gentle heat until simmering. To serve, spread the sauce over the base of 4 warm plates and put a baked pepper in the centre.

Useful tips - this recipe can be served as a starter or a main course. If baby peppers are not available use the normal sized ones but to serve as a starter cut them in half lengthways, fill and bake as directed in the recipe. The combined flavours are excellent, the appearance is pleasing and the preparation is short - very "Lazy Cook".

Venison sausages with aubergine and bacon cooked in an apple and cranberry sauce and served with two cabbages - serves 4

4 venison sausages
4 thin slices of aubergine - cut lengthwise
4 thick slices of unsmoked bacon - rind removed
4 ozs apple juice
4 ozs white wine
1 tbls. cranberry sauce

Set oven at gas 6/450f/220c/Aga roasting oven. Wrap each sausage in a slice of aubergine then a slice of bacon, secure with a wooden cocktail stick and place in an ovenproof dish. Add half the apple juice and bake in the preset oven for 10mins, cover with foil and bake for a further 30-45mins, remove from pan and keep warm. Add the remaining apple juice and wine to the pan juices and boil to reduce a little before stirring in the cranberry sauce. To serve, place the sausage parcels down the centre of a hot serving dish and glaze with a tablespoon of the sauce and edge one side with baked red cabbage and the other side with curly cabbage. Serve remaining sauce separately.

Useful tips - Venison sausages are usually available at Christmastime, but if not use any gamey sausages. For vegetarians use vegetarian sausages, roll them in a strip of leek then the aubergine.

Baked red cabbage - Recipe on page 27.

Curly cabbage

Slice and wash the cabbage and boil in a little water until it begins to soften, stirring occasionally so that all the cabbage is evenly cooked. Strain off the water, add a few twists of freshly ground white pepper and stir over a gentle heat until all moisture has evaporated. Serve.

Useful tips - curly cabbage is, I believe, superior to any other of the winter cabbages. It has an interesting texture and the colours are so brilliant and the flavour excellent. I often cook this cabbage with the addition of a little fresh orange juice and orange zest, stir in at the drying off stage, it adds even more flavour and colour. A whole cabbage can be cooked and stored covered, in a fridge. Reheat over a gentle heat stirring in orange juice, or a little butter, the latter will sharpen the colours as well as adding flavour.

Duchesse potatoes - makes 8-10

800gms (2 lb) potatoes - boiled
25gms (1oz) butter
1-2 tbls single cream or top of milk
freshly grated nutmeg
1 egg - whisked

Set oven gas 6/450f/220c/Aga baking oven.
Strain water from the potatoes, add butter, cream and lots of freshly grated nutmeg and mash until smooth. Drop from a tablespoon on to a lightly

oiled baking sheet, shape into pyramids and marking with a fork. Before baking lightly brush with whisked egg. Bake in a hot oven until brown.

Useful tips - this is another recipe which can be prepared in advance and stored, covered, before baking. For a more professional presentation, the creamed potato can be piped on to the baking sheet using a large star piping nozzle. Before doing this the creamed potato must be pressed through a sieve or Baby Moulis otherwise it will become a frustrating task as lumps will block the nozzle of the pipe.

Lemon sorbet
4 lemons
200gms (8ozs) granulated sugar
20ozs (ipt) water
2 egg whites

Peel the zest from the lemons and put in a large pan with the sugar and water, bring to boil stirring continuously until the sugar has dissolved. Boil rapidly for 6mins. remove from heat and add the juice from the lemons and when cold put into a plastic or suitable container with a lid and freeze until it begins to set. Whisk the egg whites until stiff, take the mixture from the freezer and process for a few seconds then stir it into the egg whites. Pack into the container, cover and freeze. Serve from the freezer.

Useful tips - peel the zest thinly leaving the white pithy flesh on the lemons. This is another invaluable ingredient to have in store. Serve between the main course and pudding to clear the palette. It can also be used as a base on which to pile a fresh fruit compote and and top with thick cream, this makes a very refreshing pudding to serve on a hot summer day.

"Sparkling Dome" - an essential for New Year's Eve 1999
to be prepared and frozen -
10 ozs double cream
150gms (6ozs) bitter chocolate
50gms (2ozs) butter
50gms (2ozs) walnuts - chopped
4 size 1 eggs - separated

for decoration - not needed until the dome is to be served.
10ozs double cream
chocolate squares or lace - recipe on page 41
sparklers

Whip the cream to a spreadable consistency and stir in approximately
50gms (2ozs) of the chocolate, grated. Spread this to cover the inside of
a 20oz (2pt) basin, put into a freezer bag and freeze. Melt the remaining
chocolate and butter together, allow to cool a little before stirring in the
egg yolks and the walnuts. Whisk the egg whites to a stiff consistency and
stir into the chocolate mixture, pour this into the frozen cream mould and
refreeze for a minimum of 24hrs. To serve, remove from the freezer and allow
to begin to thaw before loosening from the basin using a palette knife, Turn
it on to a serving dish and spread or pipe with whipped cream, "spike" with
chocolate squares or lace and sparklers. Light the sparklers and carry to
the table, remove sparklers before slicing to serve.

Useful tips - This is a most useful pudding to have in store to serve with or
without the sparklers. I allow it to begin to thaw in the fridge and after about
an hour I remove it from the basin and allow it thaw completely, test by
sticking a skewer into it, I promise you it will not collapse. Sparklers,
especially produced for serving with food, can be purchased from specialist
shops, get in a supply before the New Year.

Fresh oranges in brandy - allow 1 orange per person
Choose small, sweet oranges. Remove the zest from the oranges and keep.
Remove the peel and pith from each orange catching any juice as you do so.
Slice thinly removing all pips, and arrange in a serving dish. Cover with the
saved juice and sprinkle liberally with brandy. Scatter the reserved orange
zest on top.

White chocolate and ginger tablets
Recipe page 33.

Recommended store cupboard

Baking powder
Bi-carbonate of soda
Biscuits-   sweet and savoury
Black treacle
Candied and dried fruits
Chocolate -   bitter, milk, white
Cocoa powder
Coffee -   instant granules
                     fresh ground or beans

Curry powder
Dairy products
Dried breadcrumbs
Drinking chocolate
Evaporated milk
Flour-   plain
                     wholemeal

Fruit juices
Golden syrup
Herbs - fresh and dried, a good selection (keep dried herbs in cupboard)
Lemons -   fresh
Molasses
Mushroom ketchup
Mustards -   selection, including powdered English
Nuts -   a selection
Oats -   jumbo
                     porridge
Oil -   a selection
Olives -   pitted
Pasta -   various, dried
Pepper -   corns (black and white)
                     ground
                     paprika
                     cayenne
Pickles and relishes -   chutneys

	horseradish cream
	Worcester sauce
	piccalilli
	cocktail onions
	mayonnaise
Preserves -	jams, honey, lemon curd, redcurrant jelly, cranberry sauce
Rice -	brown and white
Spices -	a selection
Stocks -	frozen, meat, poultry, fish
Sugars -	granulated, demerera, dark cane, icing, caster, coffee crystals
Tomatoes-	tins (all sizes)
	purée
	sundried (in oil)
Trifle sponges	
Vinegar -	wine, cider, malt
Wine, spirits and liqueurs	

Recommended equipment

A food processor is as essential for lazy cooking as is a passport for travel abroad, if you do not possess one, may I suggest you place it at the top of your Christmas list.

In addition, a good chopping board and several sharp knives, a selection of pots and pans and casseroles, of the best quality you can afford. Other standard equipment should include, baking sheets and cooling trays, a grater, various spoons and ladles, a measuring jug, wooden spoons and spatulas.

A variety of attractive serving dishes and plates - first impressions are important and good presentation is one of the secrets of success. Presentation does not have to be elaborate, often the simplest is the most eye-catching. Never overcrowd ingredients on to too small a plate. Take Granny's old plates and dishes out of the cupboard and use them to show off your lovely meals.

Weights and measures

25 gms	= 1 oz		5 ozs	= quarter pint (1 gill)
50 gms	= 2 ozs		10 ozs	= half pint
100 gms	= 4 ozs		15 ozs	= threequarters pint
200 gms	= 8 ozs		20 ozs	= 1 pint
400 gms	= 16 ozs (1 lb)		half a litre	= 17½ ozs
800 gms	= 32 ozs (2 lbs)		1 litre	= 35 ozs
1 kg	= 2 lbs 4 ozs			

Oven temperatures

These can vary considerably and the temperatures given below, and the ones quoted in the recipes, should be used as guidelines and adjusted according to your cooker.

	Gas	F	C	Aga
Warm	1 - 2	25 - 250	10 - 120	Bottom left (4-oven)
Moderate/ simmering	3 - 4	250 - 350	120 - 160	Top left (4-oven)
Baking	4 - 5	375 - 400	180 - 200	Top (2-oven) Bottom right (4-oven)
Roasting	6 - 7	450 - 500	220 - 250	Top (2-oven) Top right (4-oven)

2-oven Aga owners can reduce the oven temperatures by using the large baking sheet, a cake-baker, or bain-marie (please refer to booklet supplied with your Aga).

Hob temperatures

Gentle simmer - an occasional bubble
Simmer - a more regular bubble
Boil - constant bubbles
Rapid boil - constant bubbles, rising in pan

Owners of 4-oven Aga's should start the simmering process on the slow hob then transfer the pan to either the top or the bottom left oven.

Complete Recipe Index

Fudge - Chocolate	30/31
Chocolate and Almond	30/31
Ginger	30/31
Vanilla	30/31
Walnut and Orange	30/31

Desserts -

Blackcurrant Trifle	12
Boxing Day pudding	44
Christmas Pudding	28/29
Cinnamon Shortbread	19
Coffee Meringue Gateau	44
Fresh Oranges in Brandy	59
Fruit Butter Tart	20
Lemon Sorbet	58
Lemon Trifle	40
Mince Pies	30
Mince Tarts	50
Rich Chocolate Creams	40
Sparkling Dome	58

Main Courses -

Christmas Terrine	38
Ham or Bacon joint - to boil	18
Ham with Mustard Sauce	17
Kedgeree	20
Roast Turkey - to prepare	23
to roast	24
Salmon Steaks with Baked Red Peppers served with a Savoury Orange Sauce	10
Savoury Gateau	37
Turkey and Mushroom Bake	43
Venison Sausages with Aubergine and Bacon cooked in an Apple and Cranberry Sauce	56
Warm Savoury Cheesecake with a Goats Cheese topping	13

Other Recipes -

Bacon Rolls	25
Brandy Sauce	29
Breadcrumbs - fresh and dried	25
Bread Sauce	26
Chipolata Sausages	25
Coffee - to make fresh	12

Notes